# THE ETERNAL KINGDOM

**TRUTH PUBLICATIONS, INC.**
**CEI BOOKSTORE**
**PO Box 1056, Athens, AL 35612**
**www.truthbooks.com**

word in the heart

6:4

# The Eternal Kingdom

## Table of Contents

ISBN 10: 1-58427-306-2

ISBN 13: 978-158427-306-6

First Printing: 2016

# Some Kingdom Prophecies

## MEMORY VERSE

"And in the days of these kings the God of heaven will set up a kingdom which shall never be destroyed. . ." (Daniel 2:44).

## I. Kingdom Planned by God

Before the creation, God had planned to send Jesus to the world. Jesus would die for lost man and establish the church, the kingdom of God. The kingdom is a body of saved people who praise God's name (Eph. 3:10-11, 21). The "kingdom of God" refers to a form of government. The kingdom belongs to God and its citizens obey God. One is not physically born into God's kingdom, as under the Jewish law. One is spiritually born into Christ (John 3:3, 5; Rom. 6:3-4).

Prophets announce the declarations of God. In Zechariah 6:12-13, the prophet told of a person whom he called the Branch who would build the temple of the Lord, would rule as king on His throne, and, at the same time, be a priest.

## II. Facts Concerning the Coming Kingdom (Isa. 2:1-4)

Isaiah foretold the establishment of the Lord's kingdom. Read Isaiah 2:1-4 now.

*A. The subject of the prophecy:* The prophet speaks of the "mountain of the Lord's house." The Lord's house refers to the family of God, the church of the living God (1 Tim. 3:15).

*B. The beginning time:* "It shall come to pass in the latter days . . . ." (Isa. 2:2; cf. Joel 2:28-32). Peter refers to this period as "the last days" and explains that they are speaking about the events of Pentecost, when the church, the kingdom began (Acts 2:16-17; 11:15).

*C. The beginning place:* "For out of Zion shall go forth the law, And the word of the Lord from Jerusalem." Zion was sometimes used for the city of Jerusalem since the temple in Jerusalem was built on Mt. Zion. The first gospel sermon was preached at Jerusalem (Acts 2:1-5).

*D. The people of the kingdom:* People of all nations, not just Jews, or Americans, or Caucasians, etc. would be citizens of the kingdom of

God. All nations shall flow into it (cf. Mark 16:15-16). Those who call on the name of the Lord shall be saved (Joel 2:32; Acts 2:21). Acts 22:16 shows that one must be baptized to call on the name of the Lord.

*E. The nature of the citizens:* The citizens of the kingdom shall beat their swords into plowshares and their spears into pruning-hooks. The kingdom will not be spread by military force. Its citizens shall be different people, changed by the gospel. They are called new creatures (2 Cor. 5:17). They will not serve sin (Rom. 6:2, 11, 16). They will be holy, as God is holy (1 Pet. 1:15-16). They will resist Satan (Jas. 4:7) and hate every false way (Ps. 119:104).

## III. Specific Days of Beginning Identified (Dan. 2:44-45)

Daniel identified the kings who would be ruling when the kingdom would be established. Nebuchadnezzar had a dream of a great image. Daniel, by inspiration, said this image represented four different world kingdoms, beginning with the Babylonian kingdom. During the days of the fourth kingdom, the Lord's kingdom would be established. That fourth kingdom was the Roman kingdom. Thus, Daniel predicted that the kingdom which would never fall would begin during the Roman reign (cf. Luke 2:1).

# Nebuchadnezzar's Dream
## Daniel 2:1-49

Head of Gold

Chest & Arms of Silver

Belly & Thighs of Bronze

Legs of Iron

Feet of Iron & Clay

*Four Kingdoms*

Babylonian
625-536 B.C.

Medo-Persian
536-330 B.C.

Greco-Macedonian
330-166 B.C.

Roman
63 B.C.-455 A.D.

## IV. Conclusion

Learn these truths:

1. The kingdom was planned by God and belongs to God!

2. The kingdom was begun on Pentecost following the death, burial, and resurrection of Jesus.

3. The kingdom was begun in Jerusalem.

4. Jesus Christ is king of the kingdom and priest over the people.

5.  Only born again individuals may be a part of the kingdom!

## Questions

### Discussion

1. Who planned the kingdom of God? _____

2. What kings would be reigning when the kingdom of God would begin? _____

3. List three actions of the Branch upon the throne. _____

   _____

   _____

4. When was the kingdom to have its beginning? _____

   _____

5. From where would the word of the Lord go forth? _____

6. Upon what condition shall one be saved (Acts 2:21)? _____

   _____

7. How should citizens in the kingdom of God conduct themselves?

   _____

8. Describe the new life in Christ. How is this different from the world? _____

   _____

| Memorize the Kingdoms of Daniel 2 | | |
|---|---|---|
| Head of Gold | Babylonia | 626-538 BC |
| Breast and arms of Silver | Medo-Persian | 538-331 BC |
| Belly and things of Brass | Macedonian | 331-30 BC |
| Legs of Iron, feet and toes of iron and clay | Roman | 30 BC till fall |

9. Would you desire to be in God's family? _____

### True or False?

_____ 1.  The kingdom of Israel was a "shadow" of the coming church (Heb. 10:1).

_____ 2. "Kingdom of God" refers to the people who belong to God and submit to His rule.

_____ 3. The Lord's house is the church building (1 Tim. 3:15).

_____ 4. The kingdom of God will never cease.

_____ 5. Citizenship in God's family demands a holy life.

## Crossword Puzzle

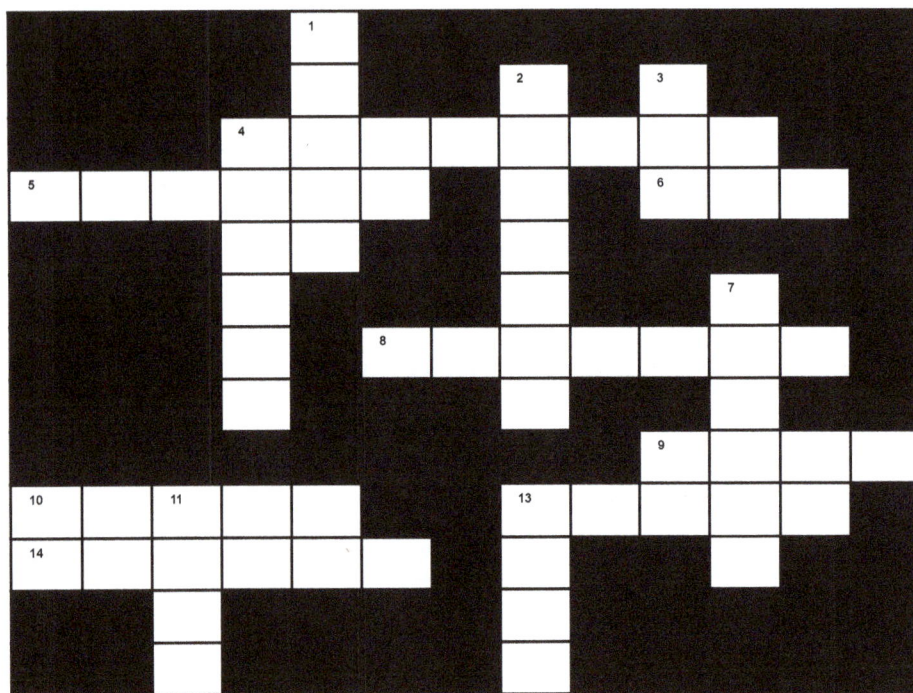

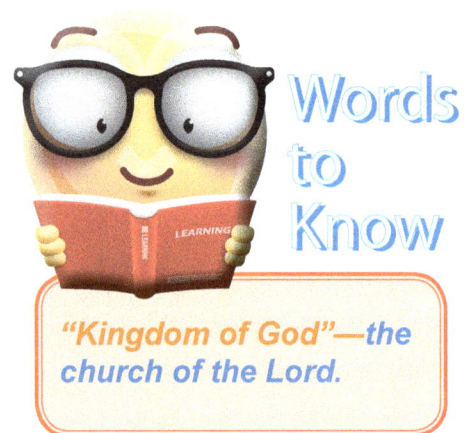

BAPTIZED, HEAD, WAR, PROPHET, BRANCH, LEGS, BELLY, NEW, PEACE, CHURCH, BREAST, KINGDOM, HOUSE, RESIST, ZION.

**ACROSS**

4. To get into Christ (Rom. 6:4)

5. Eternal purpose of God

6. Swords and Spears

8. Announce declarations of God

9. Mount of Jerusalem

10. Macedonian kingdom

12. Top of Mountains

13. Medo-Persian kingdom

**DOWN**

1. Plowshares and pruninghooks

2. System of government

3. Creatures in Christ (2 Cor. 5:17)

4. Will build temple (Zech. 6:12-13)

7. How to stop Satan (Jas. 4:7)

11. Roman Kingdom

12. Babylonian kingdom

# Preparation of the Kingdom

Jesus came into the world to save sinners (Matt. 1:21). Sin separates one from God (Isa. 59:1-8) and all have sinned (Rom. 3:23). Without Jesus coming, all of mankind would be lost. What motivated Christ to come to this world was His desire to save mankind from the damnation of sin.

The kingdom of God, which God intended to establish through Jesus, is one of justice and judgment (Ps. 89:14). Its citizens walk as God walks (1 Pet. 1:15). They beat their swords into plowshares (Isa. 2:4). Evil living is put to death (Col. 3:5).

To prepare the people for the kingdom, God sent men to preach.

**Lesson Objective:** To show the work of John the Baptist and the apostles in preparing for the establishment of the Lord's kingdom.

## I. John the Baptist

When the angel announced the birth of John, Zacharias and Elizabeth were very old (Luke 1:18). God sent John into the world to prepare people for the coming of the Christ and to testify of Christ (John 1:6). John was a good man (Luke 1:15) and God had a work for him.

*A. John's mission.* John would prepare a people for the Lord. He would turn their hearts to God (Luke 1:16-17). John was a herald, much like a town-crier. God identified the Christ to him (John 1:33-34). Jesus of Nazareth was the Christ.

*B. John's teaching.*

1. "Believe on him which would come after him, that is, on Christ Jesus" (Acts 19:4).

2. "Repent ye, for the kingdom of heaven is at hand" (Matt. 3:2). Repentance involves changing one's mind and ways (Matt. 3:8). One must quit the practice of sin to enter the kingdom of heaven.

3. God sent John to baptize (John 1:33). He baptized in Aenon because "much water" was there (John 3:23). Bible baptism is always administered by immersing the candidate. John baptized for the remission of sins (Mark 1:4).

**MEMORY VERSE**

In those days John the Baptist came preaching in the wilderness of Judea, and saying, "Repent, for the kingdom of heaven is at hand!" (Matthew 3:1-2).

4. " . . . The kingdom of heaven is at hand" ("has come near," NASB, Matt. 3:2).

## II. The Seventy

On one occasion, Jesus sent out seventy men to the villages in Galilee (Luke 10:1-20). They spoke a divine message that the kingdom of God was soon to be established (Luke 10:9). Therefore, the people needed to repent (Luke 10:11-15).

In the first century, when John and the disciples of Jesus announced the coming of the kingdom, God was speaking through His servants (Luke 10:16). Today, God speaks through His law (Gal. 1:6-12; 2 Tim. 3:16-17). When one reads the Bible, he is not reading an ordinary book. He is reading God's book!

The seventy rejoiced because of the miracles that they had performed to confirm the message they had preached. However, Jesus told them to rejoice that their names were written in heaven (Luke 10:20). Citizens of the heavenly kingdom have their names written in heaven (Heb. 12:23).

## III. The Limited Commission

The twelve apostles and the seventy were sent on a "limited" commission (Matt. 10:1-15), i.e., only to the Jews (Matt. 10:5-6). After His resurrection, Jesus sent the apostles on a second commission. It was called the "Great Commission" because its message was to be preached to every creature under heaven, not limited to the Jews (Mark 16:15-16).

The apostles preached, "The kingdom of heaven is at hand" (Matt. 10:7). The kingdom of heaven is different from earthly kingdoms (John 18:36). It is not established by military power. It is established through the preaching of the gospel. The kingdom of God is composed of righteous men (Matt. 5:20; Rom. 14:17).

## Conclusion

Before one can be in the kingdom of God, he must be "born again" (John 3:3, 5). This new birth makes one a "new creature" (2 Cor. 5:17). He is "united" with Christ (Rom. 6:5, ASV). So, the

Lord's kingdom is not identified by geographical territory with a capital city and a standing army. The kingdom of God is a spiritual kingdom, "within you" (Luke 17:20-21).

When John the Baptist, the seventy, and the apostles preached, some people wanted to be part of this kingdom. And they still do! Christians need to present the kingdom to them. Wouldn't you enjoy being in the Lord's kingdom?

## Questions

### Fill in the Blanks

1. "And she will bring forth a Son, and you shall call His name _____, for He will _____ His people from their sins" (Matt. 1:21).

2. "For _____ have sinned, and fall short of the glory of God" (Rom. 3:23).

3. "I did not know Him, but He who sent me to baptize with _____ said to me, 'Upon whom you see the _____ descending, and remaining on Him, this is He who baptizes with the Holy Spirit.' And I have seen and testified that this is the _____ of _____" (John 1:33-34).

4. "In those days John the Baptist came preaching in the wilderness of Judea, and saying, '_____, for the _____ of heaven is at hand!'" (Matt. 3:1-2).

5. "Jesus answered, 'My _____ is not of this world. . .'" (John 18:36).

6. ". . . For the kingdom of God is not eating and drinking, but _____ and _____ and _____ in the Holy Spirit" (Rom. 14:17).

### Multiple Choice

_____ 1. The kingdom of God is (a) land area; (b) military power, sword, hatred; (c) righteous people.

_____ 2. John the Baptist preached in (a) Galilee; (b) Judea; (c) Samaria.

_____ 3. When one reads the Bible, he is reading the words of (a) men; (b) angels; (c) God.

_____ 4. The "great" commission was to (a) all creatures; (b) Jews only; (c) Gentiles only.

## Complete the Following

1. Why must one repent?_____

2. What does the phrase, "at hand," mean? _____

   _____

3. List four topics in John's preaching.

   a. _____

   b. _____

   c. _____

   d. _____

4. Whose names are "written in heaven"? _____

   _____

5. Where is the kingdom of God (Luke 17:20-21)? _____

   _____

## Match the Following

_____ 1. Herald                     a. Apostles

_____ 2. Preached in Galilee        b. God

_____ 3. Limited Commission         c. Near

_____ 4. Change minds and ways      d. Bible

_____ 5. Sent John to baptize       e. Seventy

_____ 6. At hand                    f. John

_____ 7. Way God speaks today       g. Repent

# Kingdom Parables

Some of the greatest lessons Jesus taught were parables. A parable is "a story by which something real in life is used as a means of presenting a moral truth" (Dungan, *Hermeneutics*, 227). The parables use common, everyday illustrations to teach truth. Jesus said, " . . . if the blind lead the blind, both shall fall into the ditch" (Matt. 15:14). This lesson is so simple that all can understand.

## I. Purpose of Parables (Matt. 13:10).

Why did Jesus teach in parables? Here are some reasons:

*A. To reveal truth.* Truth is often understood by the use of plain, simple illustrations. Nathan gave an illustration or parable to convict David of his sin with Bathsheba (2 Sam. 12:1-6).

*B. To conceal truth.* Some were not ready for the truth. Some were against Christ. Jesus clothed His marvelous teachings in a parable to conceal the truth from His enemies, while revealing it to His disciples. The natural man cannot understand the truth of God (1 Cor. 2:14).

*3. To make the truth easily remembered.* A parable is indelibly written on one's mind. One may forget the cities of refuge, but he will not forget the parable of the sower.

*4. To cause men to agree with truth.* Parables are usually easy to understand. When the spiritual truth is explained, one should accept it.

## II. Parable of the Sower (Matt. 13:3-23): Reaction to the Word of God.

*A. The SOWER is any teacher of the word of God.* Each Christian has the duty of sowing the seed of the kingdom (Heb. 5:12).

*B. The SEED is the word of God (Luke 8:11).* Seed will reproduce only after its kind (Gen. 1:11-12). If one plants corn, he will reap corn. When the word of God was taught, "the disciples were called Christians" (Acts 11:26).

**Lesson Objective:**
To show the purpose for using parables and some of the parables Jesus used in teaching about the kingdom.

**MEMORY VERSE**

"But he who received seed on the good ground is he who hears the word and understands it. . ." (Matthew 13:23).

*C. The different SOILS represent the different kind of hearts of men.*

1. **Wayside soil** is the path which leads into the field. The soil is beaten down and hard, as a result of which the seed cannot take root. The birds devour the seed. The seed does not grow into a plant! Satan removes the word by presenting difficulties (Matt. 13:19). He uses many devices (2 Cor. 2:11).

2. **Stony soil** has no depth. The plant's roots cannot penetrate the stone to find the moisture it needs to grow. The sun scorches the plant. The plant dies! Tribulation, persecution, hardship, and offenses overthrow the faith of some (Matt. 13:20-21). Being a Christian requires more spiritual commitment than some are willing to make.

3. **Thorny soil** grows weeds that choke the plant. The plant does not produce fruit because the weeds retard its growth! The cares of the world and the deceitfulness of riches choke the word (Matt. 13:22).

4. **Good soil** allows the planted seed to grow to maturity and produce fruit! Where no hindrances are present, God will be glorified (Matt. 13:23).

## III. Parable of the Tares (Matt. 13:24-30, 36-43): The Results of False Teaching.

In this parable, an enemy of the field owner sows weeds along with good seed.

| | |
|---|---|
| Sower | Son of Man (Matt. 13:37) |
| Field | World (Matt. 13:38) |
| Good Seed | Children of Kingdom (Matt. 13:38) |
| Tares | Children of Wicked One (Matt. 13:38) |
| Enemy | Devil (Matt. 13:39) |
| Harvest | End of World (Matt. 13:39) |
| Reapers | Angels (Matt. 13:39) |

Children of the devil are produced by false teaching (impure seed). The lesson is that the word of God must be kept pure (Gal. 1:6-9; 2 John 9). Teaching false doctrines is like planting tares among the wheat.

## IV. Parable of the Mustard Seed (Matt. 13:31-32). The Growth of the Kingdom.
The mustard seed is very small. Jesus predicts the kingdom would begin small, but would grow into a large bush. The early church grew very rapidly (Acts 2:41; 4:4).

## V. Parable of Leaven (Matt. 13:33): The Spreading Influence of the Kingdom.
Yeast (leaven) is mixed in with bread dough to make the dough rise. In the same way that leaven affects dough, the Christian is to influence those around him. One's influence must be used for God. You are the salt of the earth (Matt. 5:13-16).

## VI. Parable of the Hidden Treasure (Matt. 13:44): Value of the Kingdom.
Treasures were sometimes hidden in fields. The heavenly treasure is very valuable. Sometimes one accidentally finds the truth of the gospel, like one who finds a treasure in a field. When one discovers it, all efforts should be made to obtain it.

## VII. Parable of the Pearl of Great Price (Matt. 13:45): Value of the Kingdom.
Pearls were very valuable, like diamonds or gold. In this parable, the pearl merchant was in search of the best pearl. When he found it, he sold everything he had to buy it. Some men are like the pearl merchant in their search for the truth. When one finds the kingdom of God, he should give up whatever is necessary in order to possess it.

## VIII. Parable of the Net Cast into the Sea (Matt. 13:47-52): Citizens of the Kingdom.
Christians are to try to reach every person with the gospel of Christ (Matt. 28:20; 2 Cor. 5:11). Color, race, and social condition should not prevent teaching someone the gospel. All nations are to flow into the kingdom (Isa. 2:2; Mark 16:15).

## Conclusion
If you see the value of the kingdom of God, then accept it. When the seed is planted, remove all hindrances. You can give glory to Christ!

## Questions

### Answer Briefly

1. Define "parable": _____

_____

2. What is the purpose of teaching by parables? _____

_____

_____

3. In the parable of the sower:

   a. What seed was planted? _____

   b. Who is to be a Sower? _____

   c. What happened to the seed? _____

4. What kind of heart is represented by:

   a. Wayside soil? _____

   b. Stony soil? _____

   c. Thorny soil? _____

   d. Good soil? _____

   e. What is one good lesson to learn from this parable? _____

_____

5. What is a "tare"? _____

6. What should one do when the "pearl of great price" is found?

_____

## True or False?

_____ 1. Parables are very difficult to understand.

_____ 2. Seed will reproduce only after its kind.

_____ 3. The mustard seed will grow into a small tree.

_____ 4. Influence is likened unto leaven.

_____ 5. The "pearl of great price" was found because it was sought.

_____ 6. All heavenly citizens are one in Christ.

## Unscramble the Parables

1. One who planted pure seed: WESOR _____

2. Yeast: VENLEA _____

3. A very small seed: SAMDURT  _____

4. Hidden in field: SEATURRE_____

5. Caught variety of fish: ETN _____

6. Valuable, like gold: PAELR  _____

7. Impure seed: RASET_____

# The Establishment of the Kingdom

**Lesson Objective:**
To show that the Lord established His kingdom, the church on the day of Pentecost in Acts 2.

## MEMORY VERSE

"And I also say to you that you are Peter, and on this rock I will build My church, and the gates of Hades shall not prevail against it" (Matthew 16:18).

There were several religious groups or sects meeting in the days of Christ. Among the Jews, there were: Pharisees, Sadducees, Herodians, and Essenes. Other nations were also very religious. India had Hinduism and Buddhism. China practiced Taoism and Confucianism. Japan followed Shintoism. The Greeks and Romans had a fully developed pantheon of gods.

Jesus was born into a world that was already religious. He openly expressed dissatisfaction with the religions of men. "Every plant which My heavenly Father has not planted, will be uprooted" (Matt. 15:13). Jesus promised to build His church on the foundation of faith that He is the Messiah, the Son of God. He said to Peter, ". . . on this rock (Peter's confession that Jesus was the Christ, Matt. 16:16; 1 Cor. 3:11) I will build My church" (Matt. 16:18). The kingdom of God is a Christ-centered religion!

## I. Prophecies

Jesus revealed that the kingdom was to come with power during the lifetime of some of His disciples (Mark 9:1). Just before He ascended into heaven, Jesus told the apostles to stay in Jerusalem until they received power from on high (Luke 24:49). He instructed them that they would receive power when the Holy Ghost was come upon them (Acts 1:8). Thus, the kingdom was soon to be established!

## II. The Coming of the Kingdom (Acts 2:1-47).

*1. The Day.* Pentecost (Acts 2:1), also called the feast of weeks, came on Sunday (the first day of the week). God had commanded, "And you shall count for yourselves from the day after the Sabbath, from the day that you brought the sheaf of the wave offering: seven Sabbaths shall be completed. *Count fifty days to the day after the seventh Sabbath*; then you shall offer a new grain offering to the Lord" (Lev. 23:15-16, emphasis mine). The events of Acts 2 occurred on Pentecost, a Sunday, fifty days after Jesus was crucified.

*2. Deity.* The Holy Spirit produced visible evidence of a supernatural happening (Acts 2:3-4). The kingdom was to come with power (Mark 9:1). The power would come with the Holy Spirit (Acts 1:8). The Holy Spirit came upon the apostles on the day of Pentecost (Acts 1:26-2:1).

*3. The City.* The prophets foretold that the Lord's kingdom would begin in Jerusalem (Isa. 2:3; Luke 24:49). The events of Acts 2 took place in Jerusalem (Acts 2:5).

*4. The Preacher.* Peter preached the first gospel sermon (Acts 2:14). Note Peter's qualifications:

- An apostle of Jesus Christ (Matt. 10:2).
- Had been given the keys of the kingdom (Matt. 16:18-19).
- Had seen the Lord after the resurrection from the dead (Acts 2:32).
- Was guided by the Holy Spirit (Acts 2:4).

*5. The Subjects.* Jews and proselytes from sixteen nations were present when the first gospel sermon was preached (Acts 2:5-11). The gospel was not preached to the Gentiles until Peter went to the house of Cornelius (Acts 10).

*6. The Sermon.* Peter affirms that Jesus is the Son of God! Jesus was approved of God by the miracles that He performed, which many of those present had witnessed (Acts 2:22). Peter did not need to prove that Jesus worked miracles. Everyone knew that Jesus had been crucified (Acts 2:23). There was no proof of this event needed. Jesus was raised from the dead! Since one rising from the dead is a miracle, Peter needed to prove that Jesus had been raised. As evidence of the resurrection, Peter turned to the (1) prophets to show that David foretold the resurrection of Jesus. Further, he said, (2) "we (the apostles) all are witnesses" of the resurrection (Acts 2:32). (3) Peter appealed to the miraculous events occurring that day (speaking in tongues, cloven tongues like as fire sitting on the apostles, the sound as a rushing of the mighty wind) as confirmation of what he was saying (Acts 2:33). Thus, Peter concludes that Jesus is both Lord and Christ (Acts 2:36).

**7. The Plan of Salvation.** The Jews, realizing they were sinners, asked, "What shall we do?" (Acts 2:37). Peter instructed them, "Repent, and let every one of you be baptized in the name of Jesus Christ for the forgiveness of sins, and you shall receive the gift of the Holy Spirit" (Acts 2:38).

**8. Changed individuals.** The Lord foretold that a new man would be a citizen in the kingdom of God (Isa. 2:4; 2 Cor. 5:17). This new man is one who has put off the old man of sin and resolved to walk in newness of life. The believing Jews "received his word (and) were baptized: and there were added that day about three thousand souls" (Acts 2:41).

**9. The Beginning of the Church.** On the day of Pentecost, the kingdom or church began. What is the church? The church is this body of saved individuals (Acts 2:41, 47). The church is made up of all the people who are called out of sin and to God.

How can one enter the church today? In exactly the same way as they did on Pentecost! They believed Jesus to be the Christ, repented of their sins, and were baptized for the remission of sins (Acts 2:36-38). When one obeys this instruction, he is added by God to the saved (Acts 2:41, 47).

## Questions

**Locate and Fill in the Blanks.** Use a concordance or an online Bible to locate these Scriptures. Then fill in the blanks.

1. "And I also say to you that you are Peter, and on this _____ I will build My church, and the gates of Hades shall not prevail against it." _____

2. "Therefore let all the house of Israel know _____ that God has made this Jesus, whom you crucified, both _____ and _____." _____

3. "Then Peter said to them, "Repent, and let every one of you be _____ in the name of Jesus Christ for the remission of sins; and you shall receive the gift of the Holy Spirit."

_____

4. ". . . Praising God and having favor with all the people. And the Lord _____ to the church daily those who were being saved." _____

## Answer Briefly

1. On what day of the week did Pentecost come? _____

2. How did the Holy Spirit manifest Himself? _____

_____

3. List two arguments Peter used to prove Jesus was the Son of God. _____

_____

4. What is the plan of salvation? _____

_____

5. How can one enter the church? _____

_____

## True or False?

_____ 1. There were many different religions when Jesus was born.

_____ 2. Jesus did not approve the religions of men.

_____ 3. Jesus promised to build His church.

_____ 4. There were no witnesses to the resurrection of Jesus.

## Crossword Puzzle

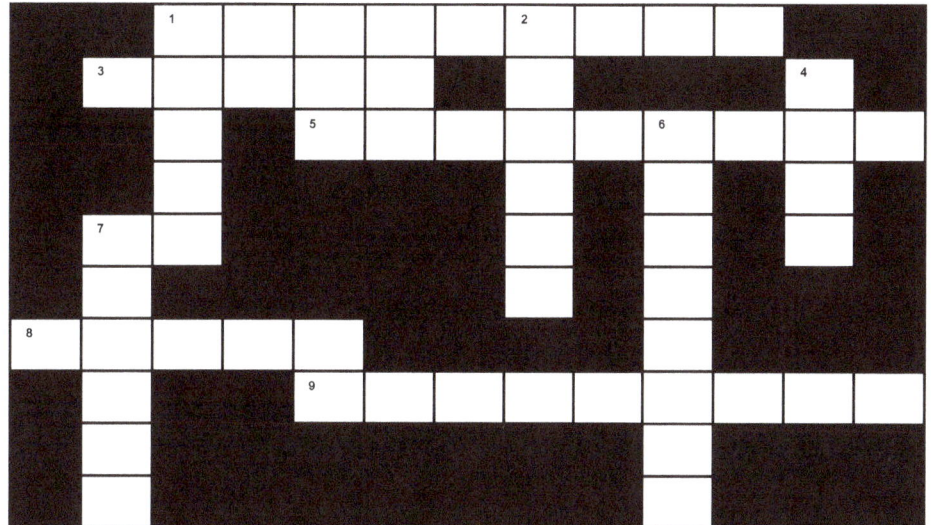

Words to be used:

**SECTS, CHURCH; PENTECOST, APOSTLES, JERUSALEM, PETER, JEWS, CORNELIUS, DAVID, GLADLY**

**ACROSS**

1. Beginning Day of the church

3. Pharisees, Sadducees, Essenes

5. Beginning City

8. Prophet who foretold resurrection

9. First Gentile convert

**DOWN**

1. Preached first sermon

2. Jesus promised to build (Matt. 16:18)

4. First subjects of Kingdom

6. Received Holy Spirit

7. Manner to receive word

# Nature of the Kingdom

Jesus affirmed, "My kingdom is not of this world. If My kingdom were of this world, My servants would fight, so that I should not be delivered to the Jews; but now My kingdom is not from here" (John 18:36).

## I. The Kingdom of God Is in the World.

A. Jesus is King in the kingdom (John 18:37).

B. Obedient believers are the citizens of His kingdom (Matt. 28:19; John 3:3, 5).

C. The territory is "all the world" (Mark 16:16).

D. The church is visible to the world. Saul persecuted the church (Acts 8:4). The "churches of Christ" sent salutations to Rome (Rom. 16:16). There was a "church of God" at Corinth (1 Cor. 1:2). In every city where men obeyed the gospel, local churches were established.

E. Jesus said the disciples were "in the world" (John 17:11). The duty of disciples is to extend their influence in the world. Christians are salt and light to the world (Matt. 5:13-16). They should not partake of the evil deeds of the world (Eph. 5:7-13).

## II. The Kingdom of God Is Not of the World.

A. The kingdom is not "of" the world. That means that the kingdom is not of earthly origin or of earthly nature. The kingdom is the expression of the "manifold wisdom of God, according to the eternal purpose which He accomplished in Christ Jesus our Lord" (Eph. 3:10-11).

B. The kingdom is not of this "world." The world refers to the present order of things, the secular world.

C. Christians are "born again" individuals (John 3:3-5). They are new creatures (2 Cor. 5:17). Three points are suggested in Romans 12:1-2.

• Christians' bodies belong to God (1 Cor. 6:19-20; 1 Pet. 2:5, 9, Eph. 4:1).

**Lesson Objective:**
To show that the kingdom of Christ is a spiritual kingdom made up of obedient believers.

## MEMORY VERSE

"Therefore, if anyone is in Christ, he is a new creation; old things have passed away; behold, all things have become new" (2 Corinthians 5:17).

- The Christian is not to be conformed to this world, but be transformed. The body of sin is destroyed (Rom. 6:6). One cannot continue to live a sinful life; he must be transformed.

- The Christian must renew his mind. Christians must have the same mind and the same judgment (1 Cor. 1:10). The Scriptures are the ordained guide (2 Tim. 3:17). People with a mind set on God will avoid sin, faithfully attend church services, show love and appreciation for their brethren, teach the lost, give cheerfully of their money, and study the word of God to determine the will of God.

## III. Dangers of Worldliness.

A. The works of Satan surround Christians. Satan is pictured as a "roaring lion" roaming around to see whom he may devour (1 Pet. 5:8).

B. Satan can and must be resisted (Jas. 4:7-8). Christians must be strong (1 Cor. 16:13), "contend" (Jude 3), "fight" (2 Tim. 4:8), "exercise" (1 Tim. 4:7), and "war" (Eph. 6:11-18).

C. One needs to understand temptation. Temptation arises from one's own lusts (Jas. 1:13-15). The avenues of temptation are listed: (1) the lust of the flesh, (2) the lust of the eyes, and (3) the pride of life (1 John 2:16). A Christian cannot serve both God and his lusts at the same time (Jas. 4:4). When temptations come, God always provides a way of escape, lest one fall into sin (1 Cor. 10:13).

## IV. How to Decide Proper Activity. Ask and answer the following questions before engaging in any activity.

1. Does this conflict with my duty as a Christian (Matt. 6:33; 2 Tim. 2:4)?

2. Does this destroy my identity as a Christian (Rom. 12:1-2)?

3. Is this a questionable matter in my own mind (Rom. 14:14, 23; 1 John 3:20-21)?

4. Is this activity destructive to my body (1 Cor. 6:19-20)?

5. Will this activity weaken my influence on others (1 Cor. 8:7-13)?

6. Will this activity place me under dangerous influence (1 Cor. 15:33)?

7. Will this activity arouse improper fleshly desires (Col. 3:5; Gal. 5:19-21)?

Christians cannot afford to be like the world. The kingdom of Christ is not "of this world."

## Questions

### Fill in the Blanks

1. "Jesus answered, 'My kingdom is _____ of this world. If My kingdom were of this world, My servants would _____, so that I should not be delivered to the Jews; but now My kingdom is not from here'" (John 18:36).

2. "You are the _____ of the earth; but if the _____ loses its flavor, how shall it be _____? It is then good for nothing but to be thrown out and trampled underfoot by men" (Matt. 5:13).

3. "I beseech you therefore, brethren, by the mercies of God, that you present your bodies a living _____, holy, ac-ceptable to God, which is your reasonable service. And do not be _____ to this world, but be _____ by the renewing of your mind, that you may prove what is that good and acceptable and perfect will of God" (Rom. 12:1-2).

4. ". . . Resist the _____ and he will flee from you. Draw near to _____ and He will draw near to you. _____ your hands, you sinners; and _____ your hearts, you double-minded" (Jas. 4:7-8).

5. "For all that is in the world—the lust of the _____, the lust of the _____, and the _____ of life—is not of the Father but is of the world" (1 John 2:16).

## Answer Briefly

1. Prove that the kingdom of God exists in the world. _____

_____

2. Who planned the kingdom? _____

3. To whom does a Christian's body belong? _____

4. From where do temptations come? _____

_____

5. Suggest some thoughts to help determine proper activity. _____

_____

_____

## Multiple Choice

_____ 1. Jesus's kingdom is (a) like the world, (b) earthly, (c) not of the world.

_____ 2. The King of God's kingdom is (a) the pope, (2) Jesus, (3) Satan.

_____ 3. The Bible reveals the church is (a) visible to the world, (b) invisible.

_____ 4. To be conformed to the world is to be (a) different from the world, (b) like the world.

_____ 5. Satan (a) will not harm young Christians, (b) seeks to devour Christians.

## Crossword Puzzle

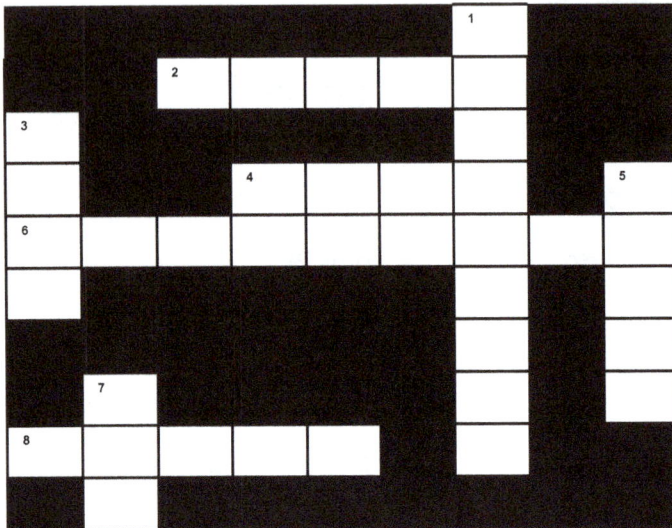

Fit These Words into the Puzzle:

**JESUS, SAUL, INFLUENCE, WORLD, GOD, SCRIPTURE, SATAN, LUST**

**DOWN**

1. Salt and light illustrate

3. Root of all temptation

5. King of kingdom

7. Who owns bodies

**ACROSS**

2. As a roaring lion

4. Persecuted the church

6. Guide for Christians

8. Present order of things

# Other Descriptions of the Kingdom

**Lesson Objective:**
**To show the various terms God uses to describe His church.**

There are a number of "word pictures" in the Bible used to describe God's kingdom. Each "word picture" of the church emphasizes a different aspect of the nature of the church.

## I. Kingdom.

The word "kingdom" suggests a form of government over some limited area.

Jesus Christ is King in the kingdom of God. Jesus said, "My kingdom is not of this world" (John 18:36). The kingdom belongs to Jesus, who rules as the absolute Monarch. A "monarch" is "the single or sole ruler of a state" (*Webster's New World Dictionary*). Christ said, "All authority has been given to Me in heaven and on earth" (Matt. 28:18). Jesus now reigns over the kingdom. He will continue to reign until the last enemy, death, is destroyed (1 Cor. 15:24-26).

The territory for the kingdom is the world (Mark 16:15).

The law of the kingdom is the word of God, the Bible (Luke 8:11).

## II. Church.

The word "church" (*ekklesia*, from *ek*, "out of," and *klesis*, "a calling") basically stresses that individuals are called out of the world.

"Church," in the *universal* sense, signifies all of the called out people of the world. Every saved person is a part of the church (Acts 2:47; Eph. 5:23). In this sense, there is but one church (Eph. 4:4; 1:22-23). In the *local* sense, "church" is used to describe the saved people in a given area.

The local church must have order. Paul told Titus to "set in order the things that are lacking, and appoint elders in every city" (Titus 1:5). The local church visibly existed in many cities, for letters were written to them (Corinth, Rome, Ephesus, etc.).

Saved people are in the church (Acts 2:47). When saved people move into a community, they will seek out other disciples of the Lord who faithfully follow the Scriptures and will work and wor-

## MEMORY VERSE

"Jesus answered, 'My kingdom is not of this world. If My kingdom were of this world, My servants would fight, so that I should not be delivered to the Jews; but now My kingdom is not from here'" (John 18:36).

ship with them, just as Paul did when he came to Jerusalem (Acts 9:26)!

## III. Body.

The word "body" emphasizes organization and interdependence. Jesus is the head of the body (Eph. 1:22-23). His headship and authority are fully manifested when He directs every part of the body, i.e., each individual Christian. Each individual member depends upon the other! Each joint and muscle of the physical body has a function to perform. So also in the body of Christ, each member has a function in the local church (Eph. 4:16). You have a work that no one else can do for you!

## IV. Family.

The word "family" manifests the close relation of a Christian to God and other Christians. The concept that God's people are a family emphasizes the relationship to God as Father, to Christ as our older brother, and to one another, like brothers and sisters in a family.

God is the Father (Eph. 4:6). Christians are brothers and sisters (2 Pet. 3:15; Col. 4:7, 9). "Brother" and "sister" are not titles, but denote relationships! Only born-again individuals are in the family of God (John 3:3-5; 2 Cor. 5:17). Those not in the family of God are children of the devil. On the other hand, sons of God are Heirs of God's blessings (Gal. 4:7).

## V. Temple.

The word "temple" suggests the dwelling place of God. Under the law of Moses, God resided on the Mercy Seat in the temple in Jerusalem (Exod. 25:17-22; 1 Kings 8:42-43). In the New Testament, God's dwelling place is not associated with a building. The word "temple" is used of both the church and individual Christians, to describe them as God's dwelling place (1 Cor. 3:16; 6:19). Christians are living stones in the Lord's temple (1 Pet. 2:4-5).

## VI. Bride.

The word "bride" shows relationship to Christ, i.e., one is married to Christ. The church is the bride of Christ (Eph. 5:31-32; Rev. 21:2,

9). Jesus is the Bridegroom (Rev. 21:9; 2 Cor. 11:2; Rom. 7:4). Jesus loves His church and gave Himself for it, just as a bridegroom loves His bride. Jesus sanctifies and cleanses the church; He is the Savior of the church (Eph. 5:25-26).

Prospective husbands seek a pure, virtuous bride. Jesus also desires a "chaste" or pure bride (2 Cor. 11 :2).

Obedient persons are the bride, the church (Heb. 5:9; Matt. 25:12). Jesus is to be obeyed because He is the head of this spiritual family (Eph. 1:22). Paul instructed that wives are to be in subjection to the husband, just like the church is in subjection to Christ (Eph. 5:24). Christians are married to Christ in order to bring forth fruit unto His name.

## Conclusion

Citizens in the kingdom of God are in the government of God. Those not in the kingdom of God are not submissive to the rule of God. They follow Satan.

All "called out" persons are in Christ's church. Those not in Christ's church have not yet been "called out" of the world.

Those in Christ are in the body of Christ, the church. Those not in the church are not in Christ.

All God's children are in His family. His family is the church. Those not in the church are not in God's family and, therefore, cannot inherit God's blessings.

God dwells in His people. God will not dwell in unholy people. People without Christ have not been purified.

The bride of Christ is the church of Christ. Jesus is the Savior of the church (Eph. 5:23). Those not in His church are not among the saved.

## Questions

### Answer Briefly

1. What nature of God's people is suggested by the following word pictures?

   a. Kingdom:_____

   b. Church: _____

   c. Body:_____

   d. Family: _____

   e. Temple: _____

   f. Bride: _____

2. What is the difference between the universal church and the local church? _____

   _____

3. What should one do in reference to his service to Christ when he moves to a new community? _____

   _____

4. How do members depend upon each other?_____

   _____

5. What relation do Christians have to each other in the family of God? _____

6. What kind of bride does Jesus desire? _____

   _____

### Multiple Choice.

_____ 1. The law of God's kingdom is the (a) law of Nature; (b) Old Testament; (c) New Testament.

_____ 2. The saved include (a) all the people on the earth; (b) people obedient to Jesus; (c) all religious people.

## True or False?

_____ 1. The kingdom of God is a democracy.

_____ 2. Every saved person is a part of the church.

_____ 3. The chief responsibility of elders is to carry out the Lord's instructions.

_____ 4. Elders are to exercise oversight.

_____ 5. God dwells in the meeting house of the church.

_____ 6. Christians must bring forth fruit to Christ.

## Match the Following

| | | |
|---|---|---|
| _____ 1. Government | a. Heir |
| _____ 2. Single or sole ruler | b. Bride |
| _____ 3. Last enemy to be destroyed | c. Monarch |
| _____ 4. Called out | d. Church |
| _____ 5. Universal church (number) | e. Body |
| _____ 6. One who inherits | f. Kingdom |
| _____ 7. Dwelling place of God. | g. Pure |
| _____ 8. Father, brother, sister | h. One |
| _____ 9. Organization, dependence | i. Death |
| _____ 10. Chaste | j. Family |
| _____ 11. Married to Christ | k. Temple |

# The Growth of the Kingdom

The book of Acts records the spread of the gospel into the cities around Jerusalem, in the province of Samaria, and in the countries of Syria, Cyprus, Asia Minor, Greece, and Rome. The Lord had foretold that all nations would enter the Messiah's kingdom. In our age, one can find the Bible in every country. It is translated into almost every language of the world.

Why did truth spread? How did truth spread? The kingdom of God is the result of the truth being taught. When people obey the truth, they are translated into the kingdom (Col. 1:13). In his lifetime, Paul said that the gospel was preached to every creature who is under heaven, meaning that both Jews and Gentiles had been taught the gospel (Col. 1:23).

## I. Reasons for Growth

*A. The word of God was taught.* In His parable of the sower, Jesus compared the word of God to seed (Luke 8:11). The purpose of sowing seed is to produce an increase. Had the apostles relaxed in the privacy of their homes, the word would never have been preached. Consequently, no souls would have been saved.

*B. Christians loved the lost.* Each individual has a soul created in the image of God. That soul is worth more than all the money in the world (Matt. 16:26). Christians see the value of the soul and work to save those who are lost.

*C. Christians possessed conviction!* The word is able to save the soul (Jas. 1:21). The apostles were compelled to preach the saving gospel. They knew the truth, therefore, they spoke it (2 Cor. 4:13; 5:11). When Christians are motivated by conviction that the sinner will be lost without the gospel, they too will work to persuade men.

*D. Persecution was brought upon the Christians.* When forced from their homes, they went everywhere preaching (Acts 8:1-4). God used these persecutions as stepping stones to reach other lost individuals.

**Lesson Objective:**
To show that early churches grew rapidly because the early saints were evangelizing the world.

## MEMORY VERSE

"And it shall come to pass that whoever calls on the name of the Lord shall be saved" (Acts 2:21).

*E. A command of God.* Jesus told the apostles that they would be His witnesses (Acts 1:8). They testified to the miracles that Jesus performed and His resurrection. Disciples were taught "to observe all things that I have commanded you (the apostles). . ." (Matt. 28:20). All Christians must be involved in teaching the gospel (2 Tim. 2:2). Some can do this publicly and others in house-to-house teaching. Public preaching is not the exclusive means of converting the lost, so one should not excuse himself from teaching others just because he cannot preach. Worldly cares keep many away from the assemblies, where they might hear the word of God. Therefore, Christians must go into the homes of sinners with the word of God!

## II. Extent of the Preaching

*A. Jerusalem.* The kingdom started in Jerusalem when 3,000 persons obeyed the gospel on the day of Pentecost (Acts 2:41). Within a short time, there were 5,000 Christian men (Acts 4:4).

*B. Judea.* A great number of people from neighboring cities came to Jerusalem and heard the truth (Acts 5:16).

*C. Samaria.* Phillip preached in Samaria (Acts 8:5, 12). Later, some of the apostles preached in other villages in Samaria (Acts 8:25). When the Lord called him, Phillip left Samaria and preached to the Ethiopian eunuch. Certainly, one with the "good news" of the gospel would tell others about it.

*D. Galilee.* Acts 9:31 mentions that some churches were in Galilee. Obviously the gospel had already spread to Galilee.

*E. Syria and surrounding area.* Persecuted disciples went to Phoenicia, Cyprus, and Antioch preaching (Acts 11:19). A great church was located in Antioch of Syria.

## III. Paul's Preaching Tours

*A. Tour One.* On each of their missionary tours, Paul and Barnabas were sent out from Antioch of Syria. They preached on the island of Cyprus. Leaving Cyprus, they travelled to south central and Eastern Turkey (Asia Minor), where they also preached the truth. Many persecutions were brought upon Paul by the Jews. Antioch of

**Paul's Travels**

Pisidia, Iconium, Lystra, and Derbe heard the truth, and many were converted to Christ.

**B. Tour Two.** On his second tour, Paul re-visited some of the churches he had established on his first missionary journey. He desired to enter Bithynia, but God called him into Macedonia (Acts 16:9). On this tour, Paul preached for the first time in Europe. He preached in Philippi, Thessalonica, Berea, Athens, and Corinth. These cities had never heard of the Christ.

**C. Tour Three.** On the third tour, Paul established the brethren in the churches that he had previously established. The Western coast of modern Turkey heard the truth. Paul preached for three years in Ephesus during which time all of Asia heard the gospel (Acts 19:10). Paul determined to raise funds for the poor among the saints in Jerusalem, so he traveled to Macedonia and Achaia to gather these funds. During these trips, he visited some of the brethren whom he had converted for the last time.

**D. Trip to Rome.** Paul's fourth tour occurred because he was arrested in Jerusalem and sent to Rome for trial. Paul had been taken captive in Jerusalem on the charge that he had taken a Gentile into the Jewish temple, which was not true (Acts 21:33). Because he could not get a fair trial in Judea, Paul appealed to Caesar. Therefore, he had to travel to Rome. There he was able to continue to teach without interference. A great number of people in Caesar's palace heard and obeyed the truth.

## Conclusion

Thus, the gospel grew rapidly in the first century. Jews and Gentiles embraced the gospel. When the gospel is preached purely, and from conviction, individuals will accept truth.

**Paul and other preachers took advantage of the good roads to go from city to city preaching the gospel. Paul traveled the old Appian Way on his trip to Rome.**

What challenge yet remains? Each individual must learn his duty to the lost. Older Christians must train the younger to teach. The future growth of the kingdom will depend upon you, your attitudes, and activities. If each Christian could teach and lead to conversion just one person a year, the number of Christians would double yearly.

"Whoever calls on the name of the Lord shall be saved" (Acts 2:21).

## Questions

### Answer Briefly

1. List five reasons why the church grew so rapidly. _____

_____

_____

2. Why or why wouldn't these same principles cause the church to grow today? _____

_____

_____

3. Describe the spread of truth from Jerusalem. _____

_____

_____

4. Who took the truth to Asia Minor and Europe? _____

5. How far west did Paul go? _____

6. What challenge faces Christians? _____

_____

_____

### True or False?

_____ 1. The word of God produces Christians.

_____ 2. Persecution will hinder the spread of truth.

_____ 3. Phillip baptized the Ethiopian Eunuch.

_____ 4. Paul had no success preaching in Rome.

## Match the Following

_____ 1. Forced disciples from homes    a. Seed

_____ 2. Christians in palace    b. Believe (2 Cor 4:13)

_____ 3. Word of God    c. Persecution

_____ 4. Spoke from conviction    d. Jerusalem

_____ 5. Paul's preaching tours    e. Three

_____ 6. 5,000 male disciples    f. Rome

# The Kingdom Is for All

Racial, social, or sexual distinctions are not to exist in the kingdom of God. Paul affirmed, "I am a debtor both to Greeks and to barbarians, both to wise and to unwise. So, as much as is in me, I am ready to preach the gospel to you who are in Rome also. For I am not ashamed of the gospel of Christ, for it is the power of God to salvation for everyone who believes, for the Jew first and also for the Greek" (Rom. 1:14-16). In Christ, "there is neither Jew nor Greek, there is neither slave nor free, there is neither male nor female; for you are all one in Christ Jesus" (Gal. 3:27-28). All are one! One person is no better than the other!

## I. The Saving of All Men

*A. Jews (Acts 2).* God separated the descendants of Abraham from other nations (Lev. 20:24; 1 Kings 8:53). God built of them a great nation. A great "wall" stood between the Jews and Gentiles (Eph. 2:14). The Jews developed racial pride and had trouble accepting that the gospel was for "all nations." When the gospel was made available to all mankind on the same conditions, trouble occurred in the early church.

The miraculous beginning of the church in Jerusalem occurred when "Jews, devout men, from every nation under heaven," were gathered in Jerusalem for the Feast of Pentecost (Acts 2:5). But, the only Gentiles present were proselytes (Acts 2:10). "Proselyte" is used in the New Testament to describe a Gentile convert to Judaism (*New Smith's Bible Dictionary*, 311). Peter preached to the Jews who had assembled in Jerusalem to observe the Feast of Pentecost. He convinced them that Jesus is the Son of God. Fifty days earlier, the Jews had killed Jesus. Those who were convicted of their sin asked, "What shall we do?" (Acts 2:37). Peter informed them of God's conditions of salvation (Acts 2:38, 41, 47).

*B. Gentiles (Acts 10).* Cornelius was the first Gentile converted to Christ (cf. Acts 11:1). Peter told Cornelius how to be saved (Acts 10:6). Being a Jew, Peter did not want to go to the house of a Gentile! God gave Peter a vision that instructed him to preach to the

**Lesson Objective:**
To demonstrate that the gospel is for all of mankind.

## MEMORY VERSE

"There is neither Jew nor Greek, there is neither slave nor free, there is neither male nor female; for you are all one in Christ Jesus" (Galatians 3:28).

Gentiles (Acts 10:28). Because what was happening was unusual, he took six Jewish brethren with him as witnesses to what God was doing. While Peter was preaching to Cornelius and his family, the Holy Spirit fell upon them, enabling them to speak in foreign languages. Peter asked his Jewish brethren who had accompanied him, "'Can anyone forbid water, that these should not be baptized who have received the Holy Spirit just as we have?' And he commanded them to be baptized in the name of the Lord" (Acts 10:47-48). Now, all people—both Jews and Gentile—had the gospel.

*C. The Jew is no better than the Gentile!* Paul asked, "Or is He the God of the Jews only? Is He not also the God of the Gentiles? Yes, of the Gentiles also" (Rom. 3:29).

## II. Means by Which One Is Saved

*A. Christ's blood is shed for all* (Rom. 3:23-25). No one can be saved without being cleansed by the blood of Christ.

*B. The gospel reveals the way of salvation* (Rom. 1:16). One learns how to treat diseases by studying medical books. One learns how to work math problems by studying books on mathematics. One learns how to be saved by studying the book of redemption—the Bible!

## III. The Gospel Is for You

Solomon told young people to remember their Creator while they are young (Eccl. 12:1). It is not necessary for you to be completely overcome by the evil world. Christ died for you!

"Be saved from this perverse generation" (Acts 2:40). Each individual must give his own heart to the Lord. No one can do this for you. Many lose their souls, planning "someday" to obey the gospel. Like Felix, they wait for a convenient time to obey the gospel (Acts 24:25). Unfortunately, most who do this never find that convenient time to obey the gospel and die outside of Christ.

## IV. Teach the Lost

Tell people about the Christ. As long as man stays in sin, he will be lost! An individual who cannot swim and is struggling in the water drowns! Why? Because he is in the water! But one can toss him a life preserver and save his life. Like the person drowning in the water, every accountable person is a sinner sinking into damnation because of his sins. You can toss the spiritual life preserver, the gospel, to those who need the truth. Do you know someone who needs Jesus?

## Conclusion

Everyone can be saved: Jews and Gentiles, black and white, slave and free, man and woman. Paul said he was "debtor" to teach others (Rom. 1:14). How long has it been since you invited someone to obey the gospel?

## Questions

### Fill in the Blanks

1. "For I am not ashamed of the _____ of Christ, for it is the power of God to _____ for everyone who believes, for the Jew first and also for the _____" (Rom. 1:16).

2. "There is neither Jew nor Greek, there is neither slave nor free, there is neither male nor _____; for you are all _____ in Christ Jesus" (Gal. 3:28).

3. "Or is He the God of the _____ only? Is He not also the God of the _____? Yes, of the Gentiles also" (Rom. 3:29).

4. "Remember now your _____ in the days of your _____, Before the difficult days come, And the years draw near when you say, 'I have no _____ in them'" (Eccl. 12:1).

### Answer Briefly

1. What is the power of God to save man? _____

2. Why were the Jews separated from the Gentiles? _____

_____

3. What is a proselyte? _____

4. Who was the first Gentile converted? _____

5. Why should one preach the gospel? _____

_____

## True or False?

_____ 1.  One person is better than the other.

_____ 2.  Jews desired to preach the gospel to the lost Gentiles.

_____ 3.  One should obey God before the evil days come.

_____ 4.  Many people are lost because they delay obeying Christ.

_____ 5.  The real reason people are lost is sin.

## Thought Questions

1. How does racial pride prevent the spread of the gospel today?

2. When should a person obey Christ?

3. What could I do to teach others about Christ?

Words to Know

*"Proselyte"— a Gentile convert to Judaism.*

# Problems of the Kingdom

The church has always had problems. In New Testament times, these problems were not ignored. They were recognized and corrected.

## I. The Avenues of Difficulty

### A. Improper Attitudes.

*1. Jewish Superiority.* In the first century, Jewish Christians felt superior to Gentile Christians. God had previously chosen the descendants of Abraham as His "special treasure" (Exod. 19:5). They considered themselves "the" people of God. The Jew reasoned that, in order for the Gentile to have any spiritual blessings, he must become a Jew.

*2. Respect of Persons.* Another problem developed when some Christians thought too highly of men. "Now I say this, that each of you says, 'I am of Paul,' or 'I am of Apollos,' or 'I am of Cephas,' or 'I am of Christ'" (1 Cor. 1:12). Paul rebukes them sharply, telling them "not to think beyond what is written" (1 Cor. 4:6). Brethren think too highly of men when they quote what other preachers teach or what the other churches practice, instead of what the Bible teaches, as authorization for what they do.

The church at Corinth also had problems when too high a regard was given to the people who possessed the more visible spiritual gifts (1 Cor. 12-14). Preference is often shown toward the members who participate in the public services. The truth is that the church is one body. Each member should depend upon each other member.

*3. Disrespect of Persons.* When problems arose about eating certain meats (1 Cor. 8), some persons become arrogant. Each person had a right to purchase any meat he desired and to eat it (1 Cor. 10:25). But, one must consider his weak brother who may have a different conscience about such matters! Paul taught the "strong" Christians not to use their "liberty" in such a way that it becomes a stumblingblock to the weak! "But when you thus sin against the brethren, and wound their weak conscience, you sin

**Lesson Objective:**
To show that churches in the first century faced many of the same problems we do today.

## MEMORY VERSE

"Because it is written, 'Be holy, for I am holy'" (1 Peter 1:16).

against Christ" (1 Cor. 8:12). Remember, one bears responsibility for his influence!

*4. Disrespect for Truth.* It makes little difference what the Bible teaches to some who are determined believe what they want to believe. One must obey the truth, because it is truth (2 Thess. 2:10).

*5. Self-Righteousness.* Self-righteous persons delight in judging others. The Jew felt righteous, though he committed the same sins as the Gentiles (Luke 18:9-14). One is not to condemn his brother in matters of personal preference (Rom. 14:1). However, teaching what God says is sinful and calling on one's brother to repent of that sin is not being self-righteous.

*6. The Love of Money* (Acts 5:1-11; 1 Tim. 6:6-10, 17-19). Jesus taught His disciples not to worry about material matters (Matt. 6:25-34). God took care of the Jews for over forty years during the wilderness wanderings and He will take care of Christians!

### B. Doctrinal Differences.

*1. Circumcision* (Acts 15). Jewish brethren would not receive Gentile brethren until they had been circumcised. Jewish Christians were binding what God had not bound!

God made "no distinction between us (Jews) and them (Gentiles), purifying their hearts by faith" (Acts 15:9). Letters were sent from the apostles to the effect that circumcision was not essential to salvation. Still, many attempted to bind what God had not bound.

*2. Legal Entanglements.* Brethren sued their brethren in the civil courts (1 Cor. 6). Distrust was in their hearts. Paul said it would be better to suffer wrong than to go to law with your brother (1 Cor. 6:7). Brethren should seek out wise, mature Christians to help them work through their conflicts.

*3. Preacher Support.* Paul and Barnabas had the same right to be supported as the other apostles (1 Cor. 9:4-6). "Even so the Lord has commanded that those who preach the gospel should live from the gospel" (1 Cor. 9:14). However, some treated Paul with contempt because he was not supported from the church funds.

4. *Insubordination* (1 Cor. 11). Women left their God-ordained position in the home (Titus 2:4-5). They desired equality with men. God's order is this: God is over Christ; Christ is over man; man is over woman (1 Cor. 11:3). This order of subjection must be observed. In the first century, some women over stepped the role God gave to them. Paul rebuked their insubordination! Today, some churches want to appoint women to serve as preachers, deacons, song leaders, and ask them to serve in roles over men (make announcements, serve the Lord's Supper, Bible class teacher when men are present, etc.).

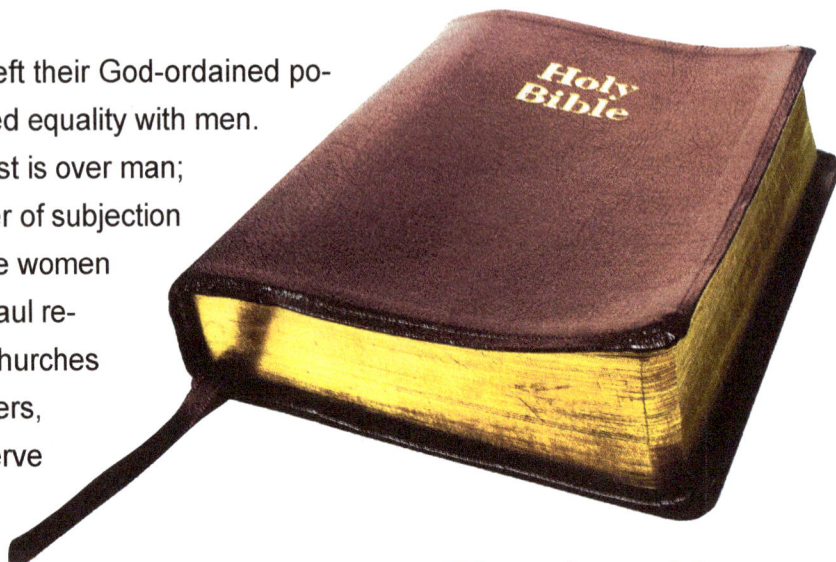

**Church problems are properly solved only an by appeal to the word of God.**

5. *Abuse of the Lord's Supper.* The Lord's Supper is a spiritual feast in memory of Christ (1 Cor. 11:24-25). Some wanted to make it into a common meal. The rich ate together, the poor did without food. But Paul did not tell the rich to share their food with the poor. Rather, he told them that eating a common meal was not part of Christian worship. "What! Do you not have houses to eat and drink in? Or do you despise the church of God and shame those who have nothing?" (1 Cor. 11:22). "If anyone is hungry, let him eat at home" (1 Cor. 11:34).

### C. Moral Involvements

1. *Lying* (Acts 5:1-11). Ananias and Sapphira lied to God about a gift they had made. God destroyed the liars by physical death. Be assured that God will punish those who lie today.

2. *Fornication* (1 Cor. 5). Christians are not to commit fornication. Fornication is a sin against God, the church, one's wife, one's children, and even one's own body. Many physical diseases are caused by fornication.

The church must be kept pure. The sinful brother should be delivered unto Satan (1 Cor. 5:5). "Purge out the old leaven" (1 Cor. 5:7). In Corinth, the sin was expelled, leading the brother to repent. "This punishment which was inflicted by the majority is sufficient for such a man, so that, on the contrary, you ought rather to forgive and comfort him, lest perhaps such a one be swallowed up with too much sorrow" (2 Cor. 2:6-7).

*3. Marriage* (1 Cor. 7). God gave a universal marriage law. He intends for one man to live with one woman. If a woman marries a second man while the first lives, she is an adulteress (Rom. 7:2-3).

## II. How to Solve Problems

What would Jesus do? The liberty of one Christian is the liberty of every Christian! If an action is wrong for another Christian, it is wrong for you. What does the Bible say? It is our rule-book to resolve moral, doctrinal, and attitudinal problems (Phil. 3:16).

**Paul went into cities filled with pagan temples and preached the pure gospel of Christ. Men turned from idols to serve the living God. This photo is of the ruins of the temple of Apollo in Corinth.**

# Questions

## Answer Briefly

1. List three avenues wherein problems arise. _____

   _____

   _____

2. What problems can a wrong attitude cause? _____

   _____

3. List some modern doctrinal differences. _____

   _____

4. How will God punish liars? _____

5. Of what problems should a teacher forewarn you? _____

   _____

## True or False?

_____ 1. God could create Jews out of stones.

_____ 2. All brethren are equal before God.

_____ 3. Love of money will not affect one's eternal destiny.

_____ 4. Preachers should be supported by the church.

_____ 5. An adulteress is a liar.

## Multiple Choice

_____ 1. Christians should follow (a) Paul, (b) Apollos, (c) Cephas, (d) Christ.

_____ 2. In eating meats, a Christian (a) may eat any meat he desires, (b) must not cause a weak brother to stumble.

_____ 3. A man should (a) make as much money as possible, (b) trust God to care for him.

_____ 4. Women are (a) in subjection to man, (b) unequal to a man, (c) superior to man.

_____ 5. The church should provide a place to eat (a) a common meal, (b) the Lord's Supper.

# The Government of the Kingdom

**Lesson Objective:**
To show the organization of the New Testament church.

Every group has some kind of organization. In sports teams, the head is the coach. On a football team, the coach tells the quarterback what play to call. When the quarterback calls the play and gives the signals, the whole team listens and responds. On his signal, the ball is hiked and everyone goes to his assigned place.

In musical groups, the director is the one who is in charge. With his baton, he gets the band or choir's attention. The starting note is given and, at the director's instruction, the song is sung or the music is played. He beats the time, fully expecting the entire group to keep up the time and stay in tune. The Lord's church also has organization so that it can function as a group in an orderly way.

## I. The Head of the Church

A. Jesus Christ is Head of the church. God "put all things under His feet, and gave Him to be head over all things to the church" (Eph. 1:22). The head is the One to whom all others are subordinate, or the One that others must obey.

Religious acts must be performed by the authority of Christ. Man has no authority in religion. It is a very serious offense to act without God's authority.

B. How does Christ rule? Jesus rules through His word, the Bible (Phil. 3:16; John 12:48). "If anyone speaks, let him speak as the oracles of God . . ." (1 Pet. 4:11). "And whatever you do in word or deed, do all in the name of the Lord Jesus . . ." (Col. 3:17). Every action must be authorized by the head. "Whoever transgresses, and does not abide in the doctrine of Christ, does not have God" (2 John 9). The church is moved by the headship of Christ when each individual Christian is guided by His rule!

The universal church has no structural organization which ties the local congregations together and enables them to pool their resources under elected representatives who make decisions binding upon the entire group and enabling them to function as a group.

## II. Elders in the Local Church

Jesus gave qualifications for men to serve as elders in the local church. Public school teachers must meet qualifications. They cannot teach in the schools without meeting the qualifications. Elders must also meet qualifications. Read the qualifications in 1 Timothy 3:1-7 and Titus 1:5-9.

There are six English terms from three Greek words which designate this office: (1) "Elder" and "presbytery" refers to an older, experienced person; (2) "Bishop" and "overseer" describe the work these men do—they oversee or superintend the church; and (3) "Pastor" and "shepherd" compares the leadership of the church to that of a shepherd who tends his flock.

Every church should have a plurality of elders (Acts 14:23). There is no authority for one elder overseeing a local church. The work of elders is limited to the local church (1 Pet. 5:2). Elders have no biblical authority to oversee the work of a plurality of local congregations.

Elders have the oversight of the church (Acts 20:28; 1 Pet. 5:2). Of course, they must always obey Christ. Elders do not legislate (or make) laws. Legislative power belongs exclusively to Christ.

Someone must make decisions for the local church in carrying out Christ's will. The Lord ordained elders for this purpose. They work somewhat as your father does in the family. They "take care of the church of God" (1 Tim. 3:5). The members of the church should respect their elders and obey them.

## III. Deacons in the Local Church

"Paul and Timothy, bondservants of Jesus Christ, To all the saints in Christ Jesus who are in Philippi, with the bishops and deacons . . ." (Phil. 1:1). The "deacons" are special servants of the church. They assist the elders in many different ways.

Deacons are assigned certain responsibilities in the church. Some works deacons may do:

- Attend to the needs of the poor
- Care for the meeting house: heating and cooling, cleaning the building, maintaining the exterior of the property, etc.

- Assist in the Bible school program
- Help in the work of visiting and home teaching
- Assist when someone is being baptized
- Any other assigned function
- Give advice to the elders

## IV. The Local Church

The universal church is composed of all saved people (Acts 2:47). There is no organization of the universal church. Most religious groups organize their local congregations into a national or international group under structured oversight (such as the Pope, a synod or council). But the Lord's church does not have any inter-congregational organization.

Local churches meet in different cities. Christians are expected to become a part of a local church and be active in its worship and work. After Paul was baptized, he moved to Jerusalem and wanted to be a part of the local church there (Acts 9:26). Christians are expected to work and worship together.

## Conclusion

Jesus Christ is the great Head of the church. The local church has elders to guide. Deacons are special servants of the church. Christians are servants of the Lord, and are under the oversight of the elders of the local church.

A disregard for the God-ordained government of the church is a disrespect for God!

## Questions

### Answer Briefly

1. What is the work of the Head of the church?_____

_____

2. How does Jesus rule the church? _____

_____

3. What work do elders oversee? _____

_____

4. What are deacons? _____

_____

5. Why should a person be a part of a local church?_____

_____

## Multiple Choice

_____ 1. The (a) Business meeting, (b) Elders, (c) Board of Directors are to guide the church.

_____ 2. "Elder" means (a) older person, (b) overseer, (c) tends a flock.

_____ 3. "Bishop" means (a) older person, (b) overseer, (c) tends a flock.

_____ 4. "Pastor" means (a) older person, (b) overseer, (c) tends a flock.

_____ 5. "Deacons" are (a) overseers, (b) little elders, (c) servants.

## Discussion

1. Why should brethren not use a different form of government for the church?

2. How does one glorify God? Relate your answer to this lesson on the government of the kingdom.

3. What happens if one changes the government of the church?

# The Work of the Kingdom

**Lesson Objective:**
To show that the work of the church consists of evangelism, edification, and relieving the needs of its members.

## MEMORY VERSE

". . .To Him be glory in the church by Christ Jesus to all generations, forever and ever. Amen" (Ephesians 3:21).

Christians are God's "workmanship, created in Christ Jesus for good works, which God prepared beforehand that we should walk in them" (Eph. 2:10). Christians are saved men and women performing good works for God!

The Bible speaks of a local church and a universal church. The universal church is composed of every saved person on the earth (Acts 2:47). The universal church has no organization, except Christ as the head of each Christian. God has not ordained an organization through which the local church can pool their resources to carry out a work larger than the local church can perform.

The local church operates as a unit, i.e., the whole acts as one. The local church has been given organization to enable it to work, viz., Christ as head, elders, deacons, members.

## I. The Individual and the Work of the Church
Every action of a Christian's life is a reflection upon Christ, the church, and the brethren. Each Christian has duty in the home, his work, society, the government, and the church!

Individual duties should not be performed by the church. "If any believing man or woman has widows, let them relieve them, and do not let the church be burdened, that it may relieve those who are really widows" (1 Tim. 5:16). The individual has a duty that the local church cannot fulfill.

## II. A People of "Good Works"
Jesus set Christians apart to perform good works (Titus 2:14; 3:8). They should be the best people of the community. Love should prompt many charitable acts (1 Cor. 13:1-3; Gal. 6:10; Jas. 1:26-27).

Though often individual and congregational duties overlap, the church cannot do an individual's work for him. Judgment is based upon each person's own actions (Matt. 25:34-40).

## III. The Congregation and the Work of the Church

God organized the church "for the equipping of the saints for the work of ministry, for the edifying of the body of Christ" (Eph. 4:12). The church has three works to perform: Evangelism, Edification, and Benevolence.

*A. Evangelism.* The local church is to support the preaching of the gospel from its collective funds. Local preachers may receive financial support (1 Cor. 9) and those who work in difficult fields may be supported by the local church (2 Cor. 11:8; Phil. 4:15-16). Preachers were always supported directly from the church. Programs of work such as radio or TV preaching, church bulletins, an internet site, Bible classes, gospel meetings, etc. are works in which local churches participate to do their work of evangelism.

There is no Bible authority for several churches to send funds to another church or to a human organization to do its work of evangelism for them.

*B. Edification* is described in Ephesians 4:12 as "for the perfecting of the saints." "Edification" is the process by which a person is fitted by proper instruction to discharge his responsibilities. Paul wrote about the edification of the church saying, ". . . the whole body, joined and knit together by what every joint supplies, according to the effective working by which every part does its share, causes growth of the body for the edifying of itself in love" (Eph. 4:16).

Elders must feed the flock (1 Pet. 5:2). Worship is a primary means of edification. Singing teaches and admonishes one another (Eph. 5:19). Prayer for one another edifies (Jas. 5:16). Proper observance of the Lord's Supper will build up spiritually (1 Cor. 11:23-30); an improper observance of the Supper will cause one to fall. Giving builds up (Acts 20:35).

Teaching edifies. Public assemblies should "provoke unto love and to good works" (Heb. 10:24). Bible classes, and special study groups are designed to edify. Sometimes elders schedule meetings designed to edify the local church. A church bulletin might be distributed to the members as a means of edifying the church.

*C. Benevolence* (" for the work of the ministry"). Every Scripture on congregational benevolence shows that aid was given only to "saints." Study Acts 2:44-45; 4:32-35; 6:1-6; 11:27-30; Romans 15:25-31; 1 Corinthians 16:1-3; 2 Corinthians 8:4; 9:1; 1 Timothy 5:16.

The church is not in competition with food banks, the Salvation Army, and other social service organizations. The church does not have responsibility to everyone who might desire some of the congregational funds. The Scriptures teach some should not be helped. "If anyone will not work, neither shall he eat" (2 Thess. 3:10).

The church, with its eldership, can do all the benevolent work God has ordained. In doing the work of benevolence, a church may buy groceries, pay a member's rent or medical bills, or otherwise help members who are not able to provide for themselves. The church does not need human organizations to do its work!

## Conclusion

The church is organized with its own elders and deacons in order to perform the work of the King. There is no need to create a human organization to do the work of elders. The God of heaven is glorified when men obey Him.

## Questions

### Answer Briefly

1. What is the universal church? _____

_____

2. Can the church do the work of the individual? _____

3. What kind of works are individuals to do? _____

_____

4. List three duties of the local church. _____

_____

5. Is God glorified when a church sends a portion of its contribution to another institution to do the work God told the local church to do? _____

## True or False?

_____ 1. One is a member of the church in all his activities.

_____ 2. Individual duties cannot be performed by the church.

_____ 3. Preachers may be supported through a missionary society.

_____ 4. Preachers are to "feed the flock."

_____ 5. The church has no "general" benevolent duties.

## Thought Questions

1. How does one glorify God?

2. What is wrong with human plans instead of divine plans?

## Crossword Puzzle

Choices: **saints, church, good, sing, wages, give**

**DOWN**

1. Better than receiving (Acts 20:35)

3. Ordained works (Titus 2:14)

4. Ones whom the church must help (1 Cor. 16:1)

**ACROSS**

2. Money sent to preachers (2 Cor. 11:8)

5. Teach and admonish one another (Eph. 5:19)

# The Worship in the Kingdom

**Lesson Objective:**
To show that one must worship in both spirit and truth for his worship to be accepted by God.

There has never been found a society that did not worship something. Man is a worshipping creature. When man does not worship Jehovah, he makes a god after his own image, and serves him. Man needs God!

"Worship" is "courtesy or reverence paid to worth; hence, honor; respect" (*Webster's New Collegiate Dictionary*, 988). "Worship" is not adoration, respect, honor, etc. "Worship" is adoration, respect, honor, etc. "paid to worth." One can offer "worship" without obeying the demands of God, but his worship is not accepted by God.

## I. The Object of Acceptable Worship

"You shall worship the Lord your God, and Him only shall you serve" (Matt. 4:10). When Cornelius fell down to worship Peter, he told him, "Stand up; I myself am also a man" (Acts 10:25-26).

God is eternal, everywhere, all powerful, all knowledgeable, just, holy, good, etc. No man possesses these qualities to perfection. Therefore, man is not the proper object of worship.

False religions worship beings other than and less than God! Some human organizations (for example, the Masons) have leaders whom they call "Worshipful Master." Roman Catholics have exalted Mary, the mother of Jesus, to divine status, as seen by their offering prayers through her as a mediator between God and man. Worldly men worship material objects. Denominationalism exalts human standards above the divine. God is a jealous God who will not tolerate men worshipping idols (Exod. 20:5). He will not tolerate disobedience to His commands regarding worship.

## II. The Character of Acceptable Worship

"God is Spirit, and those who worship Him must worship in spirit and truth" (John 4:24). Joshua encouraged the Jews to serve God "in sincerity and truth" (Josh. 24:14).

God does not accept mere outward forms of worship. The heart must accompany an individual's worship. "These people draw near

## MEMORY VERSE

"God is Spirit, and those who worship Him must worship in spirit and truth" (John 4:24).

to Me with their mouth, And honor Me with their lips, But their heart is far from Me" (Matt. 15:8).

The spirit is that part of man made in the image of God! The spirit must act in worship in order to reach the throne of God with praises. A parrot can be taught to sing and talk, but it cannot offer worship. The worship of Christians must be more than outward expressions.

Many practices during the worship assembly distract others from spiritual worship.

- Whispering during the assembly is disrespectful to God, Christ, your parents (who taught you better), your neighbors (who are attempting to worship), and to yourself. It manifests that you are disinterested in all that is being done.

- Note passing is but a quieter practice of the same error.

- Gazing at no particular object and letting the mind wander is wrong. It reflects a lack of interest in what is happening in worship.

- Texting on a phone

- Playing computer games

- Sleeping during worship

- Doing homework

- Reading secular literature

- Going to the restroom because one is not interested in the lesson

Some attend church to see the fashion show and miss the worship entirely. Can you think of other practices which manifest an improper attitude during worship?

Simply attending worship is not enough. One must involve his spirit in his worship.

## III. The Standard of Worship

God must be worshipped in spirit and in truth (John 4:24). The Bible is the basis of truth (John 17:17). Baptized disciples "continued steadfastly in the apostles' doctrine and fellowship, in the breaking of bread, and in prayers" (Acts 2:42).

Either God has a pattern for His worship or He does not. If there is a pattern of worship, man must respect that pattern in offering his worship. If there is no pattern, man may worship any manner he chooses. The Bible teaches that God has revealed how men are to worship Him.

- *Apostles' doctrine* is the teaching in the church. The gospel lessons in the assembly must conform to the Scriptures. Edification of the members occurs through the teaching in the worship assembly. Bible classes are also a means of edification.

- *Fellowship* is a joint-relation between individuals. In this context, "fellowship" refers to the sharing of the financial responsibilities in the church through the common collection on the Lord's day (1 Cor. 16:1-2).

- *Breaking of bread is the Lord's Supper.* Since unleavened bread was used in the Passover observance, we know that it was used when the Lord's Supper was instituted (Matt. 26:17). "Fruit of the vine" refers to grape juice (Matt. 26:26-29). Christians partake of the Lord's Supper on the first day of the week (Acts 20:7). It is very important that one's mind be focused on remembering what Christ did for our salvation while partaking of the Lord's Supper (1 Cor. 11:27-29).

- *Prayer* is proper at all times (1 Thess. 5:17). Man prays because he is dependent upon God !

- *Singing* is included in the worship of the local church (Eph. 5:18-19; Col. 3:16). Through singing, saints teach and admonish one another.

God demands that these items be observed regularly. Each Christian should participate in these acts of worship every Sunday (Acts 20:7).

Truth demands that these items be observed without addition or subtraction (2 John 9). For example, one sins when he adds corn bread to the Lord's table; so also, one sins when he adds mechanical instruments of music to the singing. When a church does not partake of the Lord's Supper on the Lord's day (Sunday), it has not fully obeyed the divine commands for worship.

## Conclusion

Jesus said that one should worship God in spirit and in truth (John 4:24)! "In spirit" is as important as "in truth." Worship because you love God. Do not neglect your spiritual duties. Always assemble with those who love the Lord. Do not practice unauthorized items in worship.

## Questions

### Answer Briefly

1. Define "worship": _____

   _____

2. Why should one worship God? _____

   _____

3. How does one worship in spirit? _____

   _____

4. List some distracting practices that sometimes occur during worship. _____

   _____

   _____

5. List five items of worship._____

   _____

   _____

   _____

6. Which is more important, spirit or truth? _____

   _____

### True or False?

_____ 1. If man does not know God, he does not worship.

_____ 2. One can worship at home just as acceptably as at the meeting house.

_____ 3. God is not jealous when man calls another "Worshipful Master."

_____ 4. A mechanical instrument is an addition to the Lord's plan of worship.

_____ 5. Christians are to worship every Sunday.

## Match the Following

_____ 1. Courtesy or reverence paid to worth      a. Bible

_____ 2. Attempted to worship Peter      b. Spirit and truth

_____ 3. Elements of acceptable worship      c. Cornelius

_____ 4. Basis of truth      d. Lord's Supper

_____ 5. Breaking of bread      e. Worship

Words to Know

*"Worship"—courtesy or reverence paid to worth; hence, honor; respect.*

# Citizenship in the Kingdom

A child born in the United States of America is a citizen of the United States. All other people are aliens. Aliens can complete certain acts of naturalization and become citizens. A citizen in the United States or any other country has both privileges and duties. What is so easily understood about national kingdoms is also true about God's spiritual kingdom. A citizen has both privileges and responsibilities that those who are aliens do not have.

**Lesson Objective:**
To show the privileges and responsibilities of being a citizen in God's kingdom.

## I. Privileges of Citizenship in the Kingdom of God

*A. God is your Father.* Those who have been "born again" are begotten by God and are His children. John exclaimed, "Behold what manner of love the Father has bestowed on us, that we should be called children of God!" (1 John 3:1).

*B. Sins are forgiven.* When one is born again, he enters the kingdom, that is, he becomes a citizen of the kingdom (John 3:3, 5). His sins are washed away when he obeys the gospel (Acts 2:38; 22:16). When a child of God stumbles into sin, "the blood of Jesus Christ His Son" is always available to cleanse us from all sin (1 John 1:7). What a privilege the child of God has to have forgiveness of his past sins and the blood of Christ readily available to forgive him when he stumbles into sin again.

*C. Prayers are heard.* God hears the prayers of the righteous (1 Pet. 3:12). Like a Father, God is always concerned about the well-being of His children.

God will provide food, housing, and clothing. A Christian should not worry about these items (Matt. 6:24-34). God knows how to "deliver the godly out of temptation" (2 Pet. 2:9). Christians should not worry or fret about the cares of life (Phil. 4:6). Christians can be serene in the midst of worldly anxieties.

Two blessings follow scriptural prayer: (1) One is assured that God "is able to do exceeding abundantly above all that we ask or

## MEMORY VERSE

"He has delivered us from the power of darkness and conveyed us into the kingdom of the Son of His love" (Colossians 1:13).

think" (Eph. 3:20). (2) Christians receive a "peace" which "surpasses all understanding" (Phil. 4:6-7).

*D. Christians are concerned for one another.* Christians are members of a spiritual body in which the members "have the same care for one another" (1 Cor. 12:25). We share each other's joys and sorrows and are available to help each other when the need arises.

*E. Christians are involved in the greatest work on the earth.* Each individual is involved in some kind of work on the earth. Christians work together in the greatest work on earth—saving souls. We are God's helpers (1 Cor. 3:6-9).

*F. Communion with Christ.* Each Sunday, Christians take the Lord's Supper (Acts 20:7). The supper is a called a communion with Christ (1 Cor. 10:16). When disciples improperly observe the Lord's Supper, they become spiritually weak (1 Cor. 11:30).

## II. Duties of Citizens in the Kingdom of God

All privileges have corresponding responsibilities. As a member of your family, you have some chores to fulfill. The husband has duties to the wife, and the wife to the husband. Some blessings are conditional. One must work in order to get a paycheck. One must abide by the rules of health in order to be healthy.

Citizens of any physical kingdom must fulfill certain duties. He pays taxes, obeys the laws of the land, participates in the civil defense, etc. Likewise, every citizen in the kingdom of God must participate in the work of the kingdom. There is no room in the kingdom for the lazy member.

*A. Walk by conviction.* God demands first place in your life (Matt. 6:33). He will not accept second place, such as is the case when a person puts other obligations before his obligation to God. Walk by faith (2 Cor. 5:7). Do not doubt God, Christ, the Bible, the church, etc.

*B. Aggressively preach the gospel.* You are God's ministers. Christians went everywhere preaching the word (Acts 8:3-4). Open your eyes to the fields which are white to harvest in your own neighborhood.

*C. Forsake the world.* You belong to God. God teaches, "Do not love the world . . ." (1 John 2:15f). The only hope for the world is through Christ, which is felt through the influence of Christians.

*D. Support the work planned by the elders.* Attend the worship assemblies and special meetings. Bring your friends. Plan home Bible study courses. Support the work financially. Do not speak evil of your brethren. Settle your differences.

## III. How to Become a Citizen in the Kingdom of God

God "has delivered us from the power of darkness and conveyed us into the kingdom of the Son of His love, in whom we have redemption through His blood, the forgiveness of sins" (Col. 1:13-14). Jesus Christ has power over Satan and sin!

Forgiveness is offered by Christ to those who obey Him (Heb. 5:9). Here are God's conditions for man's salvation:

- Believe in Christ and His gospel (Mark 16:15-16).
- Repent of your sins (Luke 13:3).
- Confess that Jesus is the Christ, the Son of God (Matt. 10:32; 16:16).
- Be baptized for the remission of sins (Mark 16:16; Acts 2:38; 22:16).
- Be faithful to God (Matt. 10:22; Rev. 2:10).

Young people are in the formative years. Do not waste these years! "Remember now your Creator in the days of your youth" (Eccl. 12:1). God desires your salvation (Titus 2:11). Why not enter the kingdom today?

## Questions

### Answer Briefly

1. What is an alien? _____

_____

2. List some privileges of citizenship in the kingdom. _____

_____

_____

_____

3. What are some duties of citizens? _____

_____

_____

_____

4. How does one become a citizen of God's kingdom? _____

_____

_____

_____

5. Do you desire to be a Christian? _____

### True or False?

_____ 1.  Citizenship is not very important.

_____ 2.  All citizens have duties.

_____ 3.  Cleansing for sin is always available in the kingdom.

_____ 4.  God is not interested in your physical needs.

_____ 5.  Communion is with Christ.

_____ 6.  Christians will not "bad mouth" one another.

## Match the Following

_____ 1. One not a citizen
_____ 2. Cleanses from all sin (1 John 1:7)
_____ 3. Lord's Supper
_____ 4. Ruler in "power of darkness"
_____ 5. Ones saved
_____ 6. For the remission of sins
_____ 7. Remember in days of youth

a. Satan
b. Creator
c. Alien
d. Baptized
e. Blood
f. Communion
g. Those who obey Christ

www.ingramcontent.com/pod-product-compliance
Lightning Source LLC
Chambersburg PA
CBHW081241020426
42331CB00013B/3255